FROM SHADOWS TO LIGHT

AUTHORS PRIDE
PUBLISHER

ARIENNE LEANDRES

Publisher: Authors Pride Publisher, 55-A, Pkt. D, SFS, Mayur Vihar-3, Delhi-110096, INDIA

Email: AuthorsPridePublisher@gmail.com

AuthorsPridePublisher@yahoo.com

FB Page: https://www.facebook.com/AuthorsPridePublisher/

Twitter Handle: twitter.com/authorspride

Book Title: From Shadows to Light

Book Content Copyright © 2021 Arienne Leandres

All other rights reserved with the publisher.

Cover Credit: Nitin Sushila

ISBN: 979-88-352286-1-4

Month & Year: June 2022

Writer: Arienne Leandres

10 9 8 7 6 5 4 3 2 1

General Disclaimer:

All pictures, names, posts, positions, places, acts, events, activities etc. are of pure imagination of the Author and does not depict any reality. The whole book is on the imaginary ground without any reality. The Author and the Publishers will not be responsible for resemblance of any pictures, character, person, post, position, place, events, acts, activities etc.

Copyright Disclaimer:

From Shadows to Light

ARIENNE LEANDRES

FOREWORD

Putting pen to paper expressing my deepest emotions, bringing the monsters lurking in the *'Shadows to Light'*; in a poetry form has made me feel more in control. I realized since I could express them, I could work through them.

Written at a time when I was feeling greatly overwhelmed and it seemed like the turbulent storm of life was sweeping me away, writing this book has been such a blessing and I hope that it will be a blessing to those who read it, who find themselves in a similar situation.

ACKNOWLEDGEMENT

I would like to thank my grandma first and foremost. She was my first teacher. Sitting with her in the warm sunshine and cool breeze that the countryside has to offer, I was taught many a valuable lesson. Instead of using a textbook, my grandma used to teach me practically. One such wonderful memory is of her teaching me the names of colours through flowers. She's in her nineties and through all these years I've just grown to loving, appreciating and celebrating her life more.

Then I would like to thank my best friend and husband who keeps encouraging me in the direction of my dreams. When my strength fails me, it's his strength which pulls me up to keep on going. He's been a part of my journey and without his constant love and support, this book would not have been possible.

Next, I want to thank my editor and publisher for making this dream of mine a tangible reality.

Last but not the least, I would like to extend immense heartfelt gratitude to all my readers.

Table of Contents

A Caged Bird

Nature was its abode,

The sky was its roof,

On boughs it perched and sang

Of love, of seasons passing by,

Of all that was beautiful;

With its songs the entire village rang.

The bird, free in its spirit

With not a care in the world

Enjoyed simple pleasures of life.

Little did it expect

What was going to befall,

When one day on its perch it

Heard two men arrive.

The little bird was captured,

Taken to a distant land,

Placed in a golden cage.

Try as hard as it might to free itself,

All its efforts remained futile;

And hence passed age after age.

A cage is a cage,

Even if made of gold;

Within its confines

A free spirit did it hold.

The bird in its captivity tried,

To break open the cage,

Bruised its tiny wings in the process;

So harsh was the pain, it cried out,

"Oh! Sweet nectar like taste of freedom,

Why do you remain beyond my access?"

Having tried it all,

It begged for mercy,

To be freed did it plead;

Its cries were like soft music

To the ears of the captors

To its agony, they did not heed.

The tiny bird,

Resigned itself to its fate,

The beauty of the natural world

To its reminiscence became a blur;

Then one day I chanced to come across

The bird, its heart in deep sorrow immersed.

Oh! To grant it freedom, my spirit yearned,

I opened the gate of the golden cage,

"O fly away to freedom my tiny bird!

To hills and valleys, woods and treetops,

Fountains and rivers, grasslands and deserts,

To nature your home, towards freedom well-

deserved."

A Walk Down The Memory Lane

I love the gleam

In her eyes

As she walks down

The memory lane

And pulls out

Of her repertoire

Tales of long ago.

There are decades

Lost in those eyes;

And as they sparkle

In delight

Put to shame

The glow of the burning embers.

A joyful memory

Finds its way

To her lips

And curls into a smile.

A single tear

Traces its way

Down her pallid cheek

As mirth mingles

With longing.

Battlefield

For it's in the mind, where many a battle is fought,

Some are won, some are lost.

At the fuming gateways

Conflicting thoughts confront

Fear runs rampant

Logic seems blinded

As the fighter is reminded

Of his past failures and struggles.

Distorted voices sound louder, closer

The echoes; they call him a loser.

Sometimes he'd seek to hide

Till the fear would subside,

Other times he'd take charge and fight

Putting on a brave façade

In the face of threats looming ahead

Buoyed up by hope

Though fear tries to choke.

Other times, he'd give up

Lose all faith and hope,

Reach the end of his rope.

Tired and weary,

Night dark and dreary

He'd just seek solace in sleep.

Ah! Sleep, nature's balm

Would make all his senses calm

And when sleep would wear away,

He'd be prepared for yet another day.

Birth of a Poetry

There's a thought brewing inside of me,

Like a cup of coffee.

And as the coffee boiled and foamed,

My thought gained momentum.

As the coffee gained in froth,

A poetry had taken birth.

As the warm liquid touched my lips,

I found a pen and paper in my grip.

As its aroma wafted through my nose,

I enjoyed a sense of repose.

As the sweet elixir was leisurely consumed,

My poetry had finally bloomed.

Dollhouse

Every little girl's secret wish,

Is to possess a dollhouse big,

So young as I was,

When I turned six,

My dad bought me a dollhouse;
For my birthday gift.

The dollhouse had chambers four,
A walk-in closet with a pink door,
Replete with fireplace, cabinets,
Sofas and beds,
Glamorous furnishings
And wallpaper spread.

There I played with my bestie
And my dolls Barbie and Chelsea,
Many evenings of my childhood
Were happily spent
Playing in my dollhouse, sometimes
With real, sometimes with imaginary friends.

And the art of storytelling was learnt
Which I carry to the present.
Fantasies were weaved,
Tales were spun,
My nostalgic childhood
Was full of fun.

Looking back to the good old days,

Carelessness of childhood and its ways,

Subtle reminder of innocence,

Continues to stand;

Though gathering dust in a corner,

My dollhouse grand.

Each Moment

Each moment unfolds as each petal

Of a flower silently unravelling;

And the eyes of the onlooker,

Open wide in anticipation,

And his own imagination,

Gaining some root;

As to what would show forth,

Is patiently set upon the mystery

To reveal itself, before it becomes history.

Each moment holds a treasure,

Like the distinct hue and fragrance of a petal,

And the onlooker claps in delight,

As the mystery is unfolded before his eyes.

Elixir

A writer's passion

Is to breathe life

Into otherwise lifeless words

In such a fashion

That it may rekindle

The immortal soul

Which lies dormant

As a pebble stirs up a ripple.

A writer bleeds on paper,

Her pen, sharper than a sword,

Can cure many an ailing heart,

For the soul it's an elixir.

Though life be ephemeral;

But words hold eternity in them

Coming out of a writer's pen

Can cure many a woe temporal.

A writer though, may fail to bear

Always in her mind;

Just as for her readers, her words

Are for her own soul too, an elixir.

Fireplace

What a cosy place

Is the fireplace!

Logs on top of logs

Are ignited,

Sparks, smoke, hues

Of orange and yellow

Burst forth,

Flames dancing,

Fire crackling,

Embers glowing,

Exuding warmth;

Souls lingering

Near the cosy fireplace.

Flambeau To My Heart

He holds a flambeau

To my heart

And watches as

The flames erupt

Devouring the life,
The very essence;
Stifling its beats,
Its cries of pain.

A heart-ablaze
Which had loved
And yearned
Exuding warmth
Though it continued
To be burned.

It had loved
In life
In death
Brought warmth
It loved
Till it turned
To ashes; blown
Away by the storm.

Holidays

Loved ones come together-

Both young and old,

Around the fireplace gather,

And tales are told;

Mirth is in the air,

Champagne glasses are raised high;

There's Tim, Becky and Susan fair,

And Robbie, Joey and wide-eyed Skye.

Cinnamon rolls on a platter,

Cupcakes on a tray-

Grandma picks up the latter,

To have with her latte.

Distinct music of guitar-

Floods the entire place,

Uncle lights his cigar;

And kids dance with grace.

The cat wakes from its slumber,

And joins the others for a treat;

Tim tinkers with timber,

While little Joey loves to eat.

Susan starts singing a chorus,

And soon everyone joins in;

The holidays advent thus-

Peace, joy and love, for all kith and kin.

Hurry! Let's not tarry

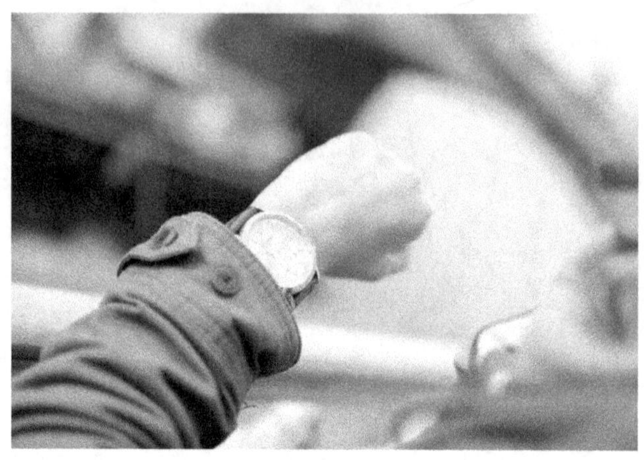

What the wind whispers in my ear

Is carried in echoes by hills

O'er the valleys

"Shh! Tis a secret," whispers

The raspy voice of the wind,

"Hurry! We mustn't tarry."

"Come fly on my wings

O'er trees, hills and valleys,

O'er lurking shadows in dark alleys;

Your lover waits-

By dawn we must reach him

In the old dome where you're to marry.

Ere the king's soldiers and kinsmen

Mounted on their galloping horses

Are hot on your heels;

Princess! Hearken to my voice-

I beseech you;

Take cover, watch out, be wary."

"You're right!" I whisper back.

"Lead me to my lover

It's time that marriage seals-

The love we've always had for each other,

Before they rip us apart;

The cruel world:

Hurry! Let's not tarry."

I've Found My Lover In The Tree

I've found my lover in the tree,

Ah! Handsome, bold and brave is he,

His rustling leaves whisper lovingly to me,

Songs of love, romantic melody.

When spring arrives, he showers me with flowers,

We meet in the evenings, like two lovers;

The fragrance of sweet flowers, calls out to me,

I rush to greet my love, Oh, how majestic is he!

When summer comes, his branches a swing

provide,

Which my companion, the wind, easily glides;

And we talk of love that forever stands true-

O tree! I've found my lover in you.

I love to hug his sturdy trunk,
When in deep sorrows is my spirit sunk,
His slender branches brush my hair soothingly,
As his leaves catch my tears, reassuringly.

He stands strong in the face of storm,
Unmoved, unshakable his solid form,
Always standing upright to protect me,
Yet gentle towards me is he.

In autumn he wears a golden crown,
And showers golden leaves on me, as I lie down
In his shade; he whispers in my ear
That I am his queen dear.

I've found my lover in the tree,
All through time and age he'd stand for me,
Our love is ethereal, we both can agree,
As he's also found a companion in me.

Just Be Yourself For Me

Masquerading to be accepted
She goes along her way,
Silently I watch from afar,
The maiden as bright as day.

She puts on a façade of someone
Who enjoys music and dancing,

When her heart is but, in a book,

When no one else is glancing.

She tries hard to appear interesting,

When indeed, she is as interesting as can be

Oh, give up the charade, the pretence,

And just be yourself for me.

You try to impress these fools,

With your fake smile and ounces of makeup

You yourself hate;

Well, now is the time to wake up

And see yourself through my eyes,

You are perfect in your imperfection,

The heart of my poetry,

The subject of my affection.

The sound of your laughter

Like pure water gushing in the creek

Your locks like a cascading waterfall

Has ignited a passion, oh so deep.

Then come to me that I may free you
From the shackles that bind
And cause your blithe heart to flutter
As a butterfly, unwind.

Let me love you as you are
And all that you can be,
All that I ask in return is
Just be yourself for me.

My Sister's Treasure Trove

My magpie of a sister

Is a collector of sorts;

Coins, fragmented jewellery

And tiny toy boats;

All find their way, shoved

Into her proud treasure trove.

Shining pebbles of varying sizes,
Colour and structure,
Painted pine cones
And a painted picture,
Mom's broken lipstick of colour mauve;
All in my sister's treasure trove.

Dolls and teddies
Of ages past,
A torn kite
From summer last,
Feathers of a peacock and a dove;
All in my sister's beloved treasure trove.

Naked

I feel your lecherous glances,

Move up and down my body,

They stop at each part,

Making me cringe.

Even though I'm clothed
I feel naked.

I feel your hot breath on my ear
As you come close, too close,
To utter something
Invading my private space
My fingers curl in a fist
My nails dig into my palms
Sharp pain shoots through my body
At that moment I feel so naked.

I feel tears well up in my eyes
As you make unsolicited comments
On my clothes, on my body
With a devilish glimmer in your eyes
As you observe my each and every move
Your rapacious sight never being satisfied.
I bite my quivering lips to keep from crying,
Too hard; I taste blood
At that moment I feel so naked.

Not in their League

Don't keep me fettered to my chair,

Within the confines of my cubicle,

Where repulsive odour's in the air,

Of dusty files and papers brittle.

Seated on my worn-out chair,

Where generations have sat year after year;

Fingers swiftly dancing from key to key,

To produce meaning on a blank paper.

Eyes transfixed on the glaring screen,

Droplets of sweat on my brow;

As I crumple under the mundane routine,

To get the task done before deadline falls due.

Labouring hard, working fast,
Unceasingly mounting stack of files-
Leaving me aghast;
This is just the beginning; we have to go miles.

9 to 5, day after day,
They call it success,
This is the world's way,
I call it stress.

A wild soul tethered to a desk,
Mechanized motions, lost my voice;
Dreams of past seeming like a burlesque
What could I do? I had no choice.

Except one day I decided to take control,
To live, not exist;
Whether they'd condemn me or extoll,
My dreams becoming hard to resist.

So, I took a leap of faith,
With trust in God soared on my wings;

With hard work reached the zenith,

Achieving my dreams and yearnings.

Now they commend my courage,

With bemused eyes sparkling with intrigue,

As they watch me rise above the average,

And realise I'm not in their league.

Of Sickness And Health

My rosy cheeks become ever so pale
As the fever rushes in heat waves
Washing over me, drowning me
In cold sweat.

My throbbing heart could do ever so less
To control the trembling of my hands.

My vision turns bleak as hallucinations
My gaze meet.

Alternatively, I feel hot and cold
My tongue loses flavour,
My feet become wobbly, as from my window
I watch the distant sunset.

Oh! Then what a boon is health
And what a bane is sickness.
Oh! How we take it all for granted;
Lying on my bed I reflect.

How I miss treading the dewy grass,
Dancing my heart out with vigour,
Savouring the delicious food, the taste
My tongue has seemed to forget.

Then, sickness I thank you
For helping me appreciate health,
For it is only when we lose something,
That we realise the importance it held.

Rain

The sunny sky turns dark

As black clouds embark

On their mission –

To pour upon the city

Silver flashes of lightning
Like swords clashing
In battle; with the sun
Glinting upon their blades.

Tumultuous roar overhead
From the clouds waiting to shed
Their heavy load –
On the dwellers below

Heavy drops of rain
Like water-filled balloons
Send many a bird flying –
To the shelter of their abode.

The slanting veil of rain*
To the world beyond – a curtain.
Droplets like pearls on the stems
Drops against the window panes

Falling slowly.

*from The Adventures of Tom Sawyer

Read my eyes

Read my eyes for my lips,

Can't express my love in words;

For words fall short when love is deep,

O what a hazard!

My eyes glow with reminiscence

Of moments spent together,

Your fingers intertwined with mine

And upon your lip's laughter.

They say eyes are the windows

Of a person's heart;

I wish, you then, could read

My love in my eyes, sweetheart.

My words may sound like a slurred speech

Of an intoxicated man,

And I'm guilty of being one;

Only I'm drunk of love, not wine.

Hence let our eyes engage in conversation

Where words won't suffice;

And may one soul reach the other

Without the need to verbalize.

Soar

I stand on the shore as a bird

Whose wings have been clipped

'Cause they said she flew too high

So, her freedom had to be nipped;

And she had to be taught

To stay on the ground

And not wander into dreams

And philosophies profound.

But they couldn't keep her from dreaming,

So, they assailed her with all their might;

And she was left screaming,

Her cries echoing into the night.

The pain was deep of

Severed wings and broken dreams

That which believed in coercion-
Was the ruling regime.

So here she stood on the shore,
Though wings clipped for a while,
She hadn't forgotten to fly
Though, for now, her home was this lonely isle.
Soon she would soar on the wings of the winds,
Away she would soar to the sky;
Out of their grasp and into freedom,
She wouldn't turn back but fly.

Reflections
by D. Annie

I SEARCH
MY SOUL
Poetry by
Baidyanath Sahay

Beats
of Beauty
Poetry Collection
By Rajul Tiwari

www.ingramcontent.com/pod-product-compliance
Lightning Source LLC
Chambersburg PA
CBHW072035150726
47999CB00002B/926